Copyright © 2025 D. LaShaunn DeNully
All rights reserved.

This journal is intended for personal reflection and educator wellness. No part of this publication may be reproduced, distributed, or transmitted in any form or by any means, including photocopying or other electronic methods, without the prior written permission of the publisher, except in the case of brief quotations for educational use or reviews.

Published by Be Your Best Self Publishing
www.byourbestself.com

First Edition: ISBN 979-8-218-72730-7

Printed in the United States of America

Design and layout by [D. LaShaunn DeNully using Canva www.canva.com]

For permissions, inquiries, or educator bundles, please contact:
ddenully@byourbestself.com

The Educator's Reset Journal:

A Be Your Best Self Guide to Teaching from a Grounded Space

An intentional space to pause, breathe, and begin again

Created by
D. LaShaunn DeNully
Founder & CEO, Be Your Best Self LLC

www.beyourbestself.com

Table Of CONTENTS

- **01** Welcome Educator
- **02** Let's Get Started
- **03** End of Year Dump
- **04** Journal Prompts
- **05** Wellness Check-Ins
- **06** Goals & Vision Setting
- **07** Summer Reset Series
- **08** Weekly Check-Ins
- **09** Joy & Intention Week
- **10** Seasonal Self-Check
- **11** Summer Pulse Check
- **12** Mindful Coloring Pages
- **13** Closing Reflections

Section One

"Teaching is the profession that teaches all the other professions." - Unknown

Welcome Educator

Welcome Educator

My name is D. LaShaunn DeNully, M.A. in Education, and I am the Founder and CEO of Be Your Best Self LLC — an organization dedicated to empowering educators, families, and leaders through intentional reflection, personal growth, and transformative learning experiences.

With over 20 years of experience as a teacher, administrator, and coach, I created The Educator's Reset: A Be Your Best Self Journal as a sacred space for educators to pause, breathe, and realign with their purpose. Whether you use this journal during the last week of school, over the summer, or as part of your back-to-school prep, it's designed to support you — on your own, with your team, or during professional development sessions.

This journal is your invitation to reclaim your voice, honor your journey, and nurture the best version of yourself — in and beyond the classroom.

Through every prompt and page, I hope you find moments of clarity, courage, and confidence. You deserve them.

Let's keep growing — one reflection at a time.

With Heart,
D. LaShaunn

How to Use this Journal

This journal is more than just pages — it's a pause, a release, and a reset.

Think of it as your personal ritual for closing one chapter and stepping with intention into the next. Whether you're decompressing after a tough academic year or honoring how far you've come, these pages are here to hold your truth, your growth, and your goals.

Take a deep breath. This is your space to reflect on what was, let go of what no longer serves you, and reset for what's ahead.

Create a routine for completion of your journal daily and return to it over time. There's no "right" way — only your way.

Just remember this: You deserve the time, and your next chapter deserves your clarity.

BE YOUR BEST SELF RESET METHOD™

REGULATE. REFLECT. RECLAIM.

Wellness. Worth. Wholeness.

Created by Detra L. DeNully, CEO & Founder
Be Your Best Self LLC, Excellence Lab LLC & Foundation

 ## REGULATE

Create a sense of safety & calm.

- take a deep breath
- check-in with your body and emotions
- honor your capacity in *this* moment.

"I don't need to push through. I need to pause and listen."

 ## REFLECT

Become the compassionate observer of your journey. Ask yourself…

- what's working for me right now?
- where am I feeling drained?
- what am I ready to let go of?

"Reflection reveals the next right steps"

 ## RECLAIM

Shift from surviving to intentional living

- choose one small act to support your well-being
- set a boundary, reset or reach out for support
- reconnect with what brings you joy.

"Reclaiming myself Is not selfish, It's necessary"

Grounding  Practice

Overwhelmed?   Let's tap Into our 5 Senses

5 THINGS YOU SEE
- ○ _____
- ○ _____
- ○ _____
- ○ _____
- ○ _____

2 THINGS YOU SMELL
- ♡ _____
- ♡ _____

4 THINGS YOU CAN TOUCH
- ♡ _____
- ♡ _____
- ♡ _____
- ♡ _____

1 THING YOU TASTE
_____

3 THINGS YOU HEAR
_____
_____
_____

My Me-Time Menu

Take a few minutes to pause and reconnect with what brings you peace, pleasure, and presence. In each section, list simple activities that help you reset, no matter how much time you have. Use this as your personal menu of care when you need a moment to return to yourself.

🕐 5-Minute Resets

_____

_____

_____

_____

☕ 30-Minute Breaks

_____

_____

_____

_____

🎉 Weekend Reset & Joy

_____

_____

_____

_____

Weekly Self-Care Tracker
(7) Days of Tracking Activities for "Me"

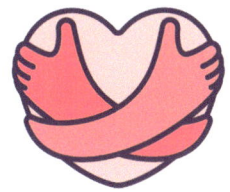

Day of Week	Self Care Activity	Mood Before	Mood After

Section Two

Let's Get Started

Start here...

"This is your moment to breathe before the journey begins."

What are you carrying as this school year ends? What do you hope this journal helps you release, remember, or renew?

Stop & Jot

Section Three

"Your story matters. Your voice matters. You matter"
- Kerry Washington

End of Year Dump

My End of Year Dump!

The _____ School Year Is Over!

Let your fingers do the work, write out your thoughts.

_____
_____
_____
_____
_____
_____
_____
_____
_____
_____
_____
_____
_____
_____
_____

Moment of Reflect & Reset
Section Three Checkpoint

AFFIRMATIONS:

- By putting these memories and feelings into words, I am honoring my journey and creating space for healing and growth.

- I can hold gratitude and frustration, pride and disappointment, love and exhaustion all at the same time—this complexity makes me human.

MINDFULNESS PROMPT:

Place one hand on your heart and one on your stomach. Feel your breath moving naturally. Notice: What do you need most in this moment? Rest? Movement? A cup of tea?

_____

_____

_____

PERSONAL MANTRA/INTENTION:

_____

_____

Stop & Jot

Section Four

"Teaching kids to count is fine, but teaching them what counts is best"
— Bob Talbert

Journal Prompts

Learnings/Aha Moments
from this school year

Big Wins!
_____
_____
_____
_____
_____
_____
_____
_____
_____
_____

Scholars taught me...
_____
_____
_____
_____
_____
_____
_____
_____
_____
_____

Aha Moments
_____
_____
_____
_____
_____
_____
_____
_____
_____
_____

That was surprising...
_____
_____
_____
_____
_____
_____
_____
_____
_____
_____

Glows & Grows

Celebrate your highlights and Reflect on your areas of growth

My Glows

1. _____
   _____
   _____
   _____
   _____

2. _____
   _____
   _____
   _____
   _____

3. _____
   _____
   _____
   _____
   _____

My Grows

1. _____
   _____
   _____
   _____
   _____

2. _____
   _____
   _____
   _____
   _____

3. _____
   _____
   _____
   _____
   _____

Stop & Jot

Moment of Reflect & Reset
Section Four Checkpoint

AFFIRMATIONS:
- My students were my greatest teachers this year, and I am grateful for the wisdom they shared with me.
- I celebrate every victory, both big and small, as evidence of my growth and impact as an educator.

MINDFULNESS PROMPT:
Think of a student who taught you something meaningful this year. Picture their face and send them gratitude silently. Notice any emotions that arise—perhaps tenderness, appreciation, or wonder. Let these feelings flow through you as a reminder of the beautiful exchange that happens in teaching.

_____

_____

_____

PERSONAL MANTRA/INTENTION:

_____

_____

Section Five

"Self-care is not selfish. You cannot serve from an empty vessel." - Eleanor Brownn

Wellness Check-Ins

Wellness Check-In

How well did I treat myself this year?

What self-care practices actually worked for me versus what I thought should work?

_____
_____
_____
_____
_____
_____
_____
_____
_____
_____

What emotions came up for me most frequently in the classroom this year?

_____
_____
_____
_____
_____
_____
_____
_____
_____
_____

What support did I need that I didn't ask for or receive?

_____
_____
_____
_____
_____
_____
_____
_____

Lift & Limit

What lifts me up and supports the person I am becoming? What limits my joy and well-being?

Lifts

1. _____
_____
_____
_____

2. _____
_____
_____
_____

3. _____
_____
_____
_____
_____

Limits

1. _____
_____
_____
_____

2. _____
_____
_____
_____

3. _____
_____
_____
_____

Wellness Check-In

How will I be more intentional about my mental & physical health next year?

What do I need to replenish my spirit right now?
_____
_____
_____
_____
_____
_____
_____
_____

How do I let go of this school year so I can prepare for the next?
_____
_____
_____
_____
_____
_____
_____

What support will I request at the start of next school year in order to ensure my wellness?
_____
_____
_____
_____
_____
_____

Stop & Jot

Moment of Reflect & Reset
Section Five Checkpoint

AFFIRMATIONS:
- It is wise and courageous to recognize what I need and to advocate for the support that will help me thrive as an educator.
- I can release this school year with gratitude while still honoring the lessons it taught me about caring for myself.

MINDFULNESS PROMPT:
Imagine holding this past school year gently in your hands like a bird you're ready to release. Take three deep breaths, and with each exhale, visualize letting it fly free—taking with it any stress, disappointment, or heaviness you're ready to release. Notice the lightness that remains as you create space for what's to come.

_____

_____

_____

PERSONAL MANTRA/INTENTION:

_____

_____

"Take time to make your soul happy. The classroom will still be there when you return, but you'll bring a renewed heart to it." - Unknown

Pause and reflect on your "why", your reason for being. Remind yourself why you became an educator and head learner

_____
_____
_____
_____
_____
_____
_____
_____
_____
_____
_____
_____
_____

Section Six

"The best time to plant a tree was 20 years ago. The second best time is now."
—Chinese Proverb

Goals & Vision Setting

What's Next For You?

Let your fingers do the work, write out your thoughts.

_____

_____

_____

_____

_____

_____

_____

_____

_____

_____

_____

_____

_____

_____

_____

Lift & Limit

What lifts me up and supports the person I am becoming? What limits my joy and well-being?

Lifts

1. _____
2. _____
3. _____

Limits

1. _____
2. _____
3. _____

Directions for Completion Your Classroom Compass

- **Step 1:** Find Your Center In the center circle, write one word or short phrase that will be your guiding theme for the year. This could be a value like "connection," "growth," "joy," or "balance"—whatever feels most important to your teaching journey right now.

- **Step 2:** Navigate Each Direction Move to each compass point and brainstorm 2-3 specific goals for each area:

- **North (Academic Goals):** What do you want your students to learn, achieve, or experience academically? Think curriculum, skills, assessments, or learning outcomes.

- **South (Personal Wellness Goals):** How will you care for yourself as an educator? Consider boundaries, self-care practices, stress management, or work-life balance.

- **East (Student Relationship Goals):** What kind of connections do you want to build with and between your students? Think classroom community, individual relationships, or social-emotional learning.

- **West (Professional Growth Goals):** How do you want to develop as an educator? Consider new strategies, training, collaboration, or leadership opportunities.

- **Step 3:** Connect the Directions Draw lines or arrows between related goals to see how they support each other. For example, your wellness goals might directly impact your ability to build strong student relationships.

- **Step 4:** Add Your Action Steps Around the outside edge, jot down specific actions or monthly check-ins for each goal. These become your roadmap for the year.

Use colors, symbols, or drawings to make it uniquely yours—this compass should feel like a personal navigation tool you'll want to revisit throughout the year.

Your Classroom Compass

North: Academic goals

West: Professional growth goals

Center: Your guiding word/theme for the year

East: Student relationship goals

South: Personal wellness goals

Vision Map

"The Educator I'm Becoming"

Envisioning My Best Self In the Classroom

What will be my lesson planning routine?

_____

How will I pace my lessons to ensure that all components of my lesson plan are taught? For example, Do Now, hook, mini-lesson, guided and Independent practice, closing (lesson wrap-up) and exit ticket)

_____

_____

_____

What kind of energy do I want to bring into my space?
🌈 Calm | 🔥 Passionate | 🧠 Thoughtful | 💪 Motivated

Other _____

What do I want to be known for by my scholars this year?

_____

_____

_____

 # Focus Map
"My Top 3 Priorities"

PROGRESS EMOJI METER

PROGRESS EMOJI METER

GOAL #1:

WHAT IS IT?

WHY DOES IT MATTER?

FIRST SMALL STEP I CAN TAKE:

GOAL #2:

WHAT IS IT?

WHY DOES IT MATTER?

FIRST SMALL STEP I CAN TAKE:

PROGRESS EMOJI METER

GOAL #1:

WHAT IS IT?

WHY DOES IT MATTER?

FIRST SMALL STEP I CAN TAKE:

 Growth Plan: Sustaining My Progress

Nurturing My Goals Over Time

- Support I need to succeed (People, tools, time)

- What could get in the way? Write it, Face It, Plan for It

- What progress looks like even if it's not perfect?

- When I feel discouraged, I'll remind myself to:
  - ☐ Ask for help
  - ☐ Celebrate Progress
  - ☐ Rest when needed
  - ☐ Reflect & Reset

Moment of Reflect & Reset
Section Six Checkpoint

AFFIRMATIONS:
- The teacher I am becoming is shaped by intention, experience, and hope —I am exactly where I need to be in my journey. I can release this school year with gratitude while still honoring the lessons it taught me about caring for myself.
- I have the wisdom to discern what served me well this year and the courage to release what no longer fits my vision for teaching.

MINDFULNESS PROMPT:
Sit quietly and imagine walking into your ideal classroom next year. What do you see, hear, and feel? How do students interact with each other and with you? What energy fills the space? Let this vision settle into your body as you breathe deeply, noticing what feels most important and authentic to you.

_____

_____

_____

_____

PERSONAL MANTRA/INTENTION:

_____

_____

"Teaching is the profession that teaches all the other professions." - Unknown

Section Seven

"The art of teaching is the art of assisting discovery. But you can't assist others in finding what you've lost yourself. Summer helps you remember."
- Mark Van Doren (adapted)

Summer Reset Series

MONTH

MON	TUE	WED	THU	FRI	SAT	SUN

MONTH

MON	TUE	WED	THU	FRI	SAT	SUN

MONTH

MON	TUE	WED	THU	FRI	SAT	SUN

EARLY SUMMER FOCUS HABIT TRACKER

What are my intentions for this summer?

_____

_____

_____

	M	T	W	T	F	S	S
Rest	○	○	○	○	○	○	○
Joy	○	○	○	○	○	○	○
Hydration	○	○	○	○	○	○	○
Light Planning	○	○	○	○	○	○	○
Exercise	○	○	○	○	○	○	○

How did completing these habits make me feel?
😊 Energized | 😌 Balanced | 😴 Drained

Did these habits help me feel more like my best self?
⭐ Absolutely | 😐 A little | ⊗ Not yet

MID-SUMMER MOMENTUM HABIT TRACKER

Where am I thriving? What do I want to adjust?

_____
_____
_____

	M	T	W	T	F	S	S
Hydration	○	○	○	○	○	○	○
Reading	○	○	○	○	○	○	○
Sleeping	○	○	○	○	○	○	○
Joy	○	○	○	○	○	○	○
Journaling	○	○	○	○	○	○	○

What habit was most challenging for me? Why?

_____
_____

How consistent was I with my habits?
🙂 Consistent | 😐 Somewhat | 😣 Not really

LATE SUMMER ALIGNMENT HABIT TRACKER

Affirmations
_____
_____
_____

	M	T	W	T	F	S	S
Affirmations	○	○	○	○	○	○	○
Morning Routine	○	○	○	○	○	○	○
Joy	○	○	○	○	○	○	○
Hydration	○	○	○	○	○	○	○
Prep Time	○	○	○	○	○	○	○

What habits support the educator I want to be next year?
_____
_____

Are you ready to return?
⭐ Absolutely | 😕 A little | ⊗ Not yet

Section Eight

Weekly Check-Ins

Weekly Check-In

"Teaching is the profession that teaches all the other professions." - Unknown

Take this time to check-in with yourself.

One act of Self-Care I am committing to this week

_____
_____
_____

What am I letting go of...	My Big Wins of the Week
_____	_____
_____	_____
_____	_____
_____	_____
_____	_____
_____	_____
_____	_____
_____	_____

What am I prioritizing...

_____
_____
_____

My Summer

Log!

Personal...

_____
_____
_____
_____
_____
_____

Professional...

_____
_____
_____
_____
_____
_____

Celebrate You

You showed up. You slowed down.
You grew. Let's honor that.

One word that describes this season

_____

Three Wins I'm Celebrating:

1.

2.

3.

A moment that surprised me

_____
_____
_____
_____

A habit I stuck with

_____
_____
_____

A mindset I'm proud of

_____
_____
_____

"The best teachers are those who show you where to look but don't tell you what to see. But first, they must remember to look up and see for themselves." - Alexandra K. Trenfor

_____

_____

_____

_____

_____

_____

_____

_____

_____

_____

_____

_____

_____

_____

Weekly Check-In

What I will be Intentional about this week...
_____
_____
_____

Big Wins of the Week   What's keeping me up at night
_____   _____
_____   _____
_____   _____
_____   _____
_____   _____
_____   _____
_____   _____
_____   _____

I am enjoying...
_____
_____

My Summer

WIN Log!

Personal...
_____
_____
_____
_____
_____
_____

Professional...
_____
_____
_____
_____
_____
_____

 # Celebrate You

*You showed up. You slowed down.
You grew. Let's honor that.*

One word that describes this season

_____

Three Wins I'm Celebrating:

1.

2.

3.

A moment that surprised me

_____
_____
_____
_____

A habit I stuck with

_____
_____
_____

A mindset I'm proud of

_____
_____
_____

"A teacher affects eternity, but first they must tend to their own garden. Let summer be your growing season."
- Henry Adams (adapted)

_____
_____
_____
_____
_____
_____
_____
_____
_____
_____
_____
_____
_____

Weekly Check-In

One act of Self-Care I committing to this week

_____
_____
_____

What I'm planning...

_____
_____
_____
_____
_____
_____
_____
_____

Big Wins of the Week

_____
_____
_____
_____
_____
_____
_____
_____

How I want to show up next week

_____
_____
_____

My Summer  Log!

Personal...
_____
_____
_____
_____
_____
_____

Professional...
_____
_____
_____
_____
_____
_____

 Celebrate You

You showed up. You slowed down. You grew. Let's honor that.

One word that describes this season

_____

Three Wins I'm Celebrating:

1.

2.

3.

A moment that surprised me

_____
_____
_____
_____

A habit I stuck with

_____
_____
_____

A mindset I'm proud of

_____
_____
_____

"In every walk with nature, one receives far more than they seek. Let summer restore what the school year depleted." - John Muir (adapted)

Section Nine

Joy & Intention Week

Joy & Intention Week

Center joy. Set your Intentions. Make space for what matters most.

- What would bring me joy this week (big or small)?

- What am I saying YES to this week?

- What am I saying NO to (without guilt)?

- One intention I want to carry Into each day:

- How will I care for my mind and body this week?

- A joy ritual I'll return to this week (music, movement, silence, etc):

"September is coming, but August is yours. Fill it with whatever feeds your teacher soul." - Unknown

_____

_____

_____

_____

_____

_____

_____

_____

_____

_____

_____

_____

_____

_____

Section Ten

Seasonal Self Check

Seasonal Self-Check

Reflect on your rhythm, realign with your values, and reset with Intention

- What season of life am I In right now?

- Where do I feel out of sync or drained?

- A practice that's been nourishing me lately:

- What can I release to feel more free?

- What do I want to carry forward Into the next season?

LETTER TO MY
future self

Dear Me,

_____

_____

_____

_____

_____

_____

_____

_____

_____

Signed:

Date:

Section Eleven

Summer Pulse Check

Summer Pulse Check

Pause, reflect, and check In with your energy, goals and mindset

- What has been most energizing for me this summer?

- What's something I need to pause or let go of?

- A message I needed to hear recently was:

- A goal I'm making progress on:

- A quote I came across that I must record:

- What's one thing I still want to prioritize this summer?

Section Twelve

Mindful Coloring Pages

Mindful Coloring

MINDFUL
Mandala

Mindful Coloring

MINDFUL Mandala

Mindful Coloring

MINDFUL
Mandala

Section Thirteen

"You have been assigned this mountain to show others it can be moved." - Mel Robbins

Closing Reflection: A Note to Self

Closing Reflection
You've done something powerful

You carved out space to reflect, breathe, and reset — not just for your role as an educator, but for yourself as a human being. These pages now hold your wisdom, your growth, and your resilience.

As you move forward, remember:
- You are more than your to-do list.
- You are worthy of rest, reflection, and joy.
- You carry everything you need, to make next year meaningful — not just for your scholars but for YOU

Before you close this journal, take a moment to write a message to yourself — a reminder, a truth, or an intention you want to carry into the year ahead.

HABIT TRACKER
List habits you feel will serve you Into the school year.

One Word or Emoji to describe this week
_____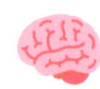

	M	T	W	T	F	S	S
	○	○	○	○	○	○	○
	○	○	○	○	○	○	○
	○	○	○	○	○	○	○
	○	○	○	○	○	○	○
	○	○	○	○	○	○	○

	M	T	W	T	F	S	S
	○	○	○	○	○	○	○
	○	○	○	○	○	○	○

Classroom Culture Check-In

What sounds do I want to hear In my classroom next year?

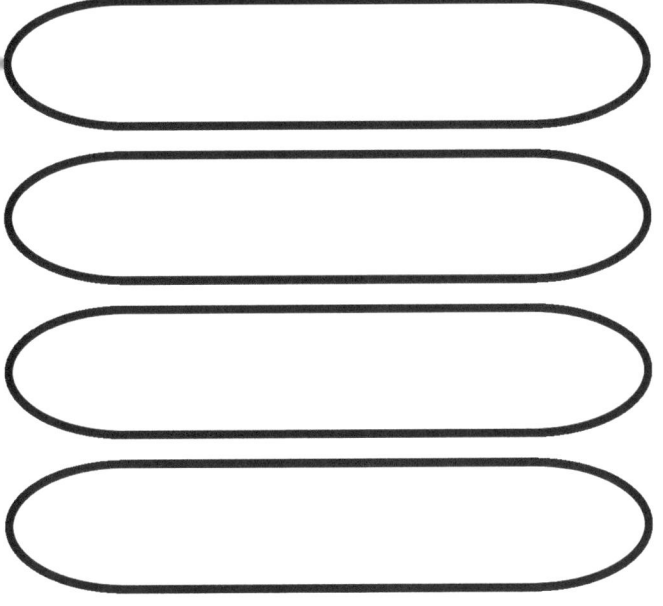

What is a must In my classroom next year?

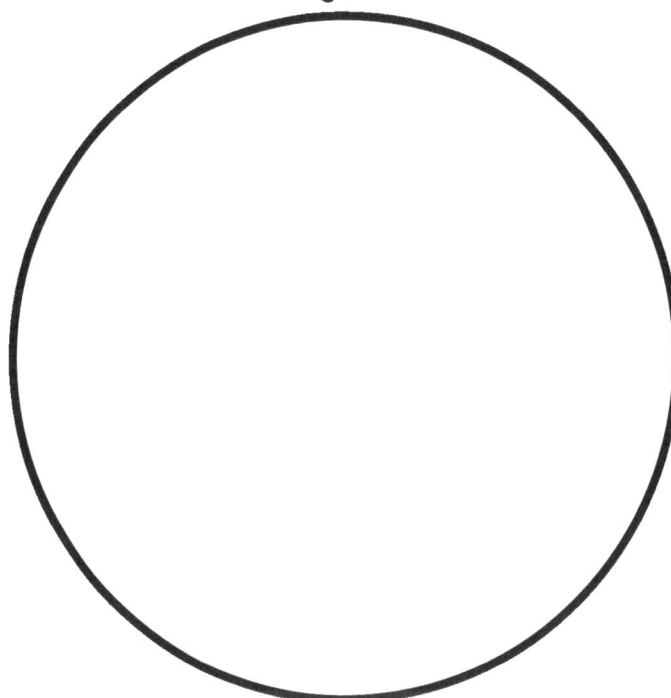

How do I want to feel as a teacher next year?

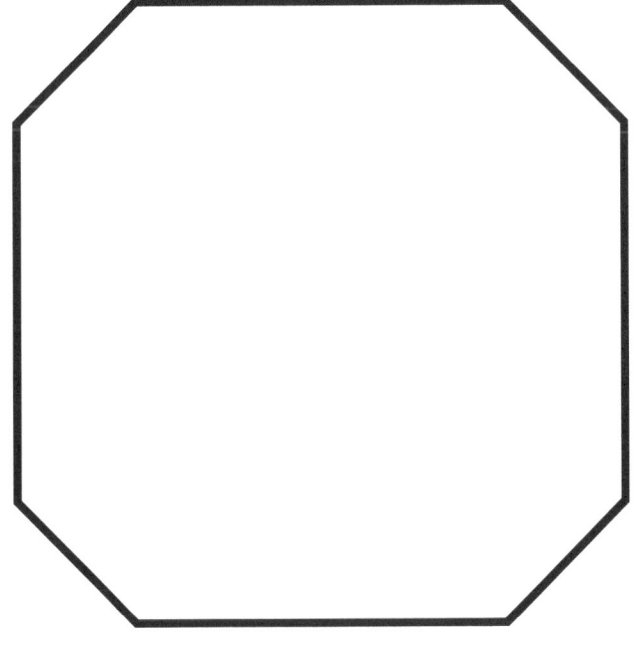

What do I want to display In my classroom next year?

"A teacher affects eternity, but first they must tend to their own garden. Let summer be your growing season." - Henry Adams (adapted)

Note to Self

Thank You!

I hope this journal helped you regulate reflect, and reclaim for the path ahead.
Keep honoring your journey.
The best is yet to come.
Share your reflections with #EducatorsReset

BONUS GIFT:
Enjoy this calming playlist Click here

Visit www.byourbestself.com for more resources and support.

www.ingramcontent.com/pod-product-compliance
Lightning Source LLC
Chambersburg PA
CBHW041417010526
44107CB00016B/1201